Six Steps To Living Successfully As a Believer

To help you START RIGHT
And STAY RIGHT

By BOBBY JACKSON
Revised by JIM COX

Copyright 2015

By

James G. Cox

ISBN 978-0-9966890-1-4

All rights reserved.

All Scripture verses are from the
King James Bible for Today.

Printed in the United States of America

To order additional copies
of this book contact us at:

HopewayBooks.com

Or

hopewaybooks@gmail.com

Foreword

Bobby Jackson was born in a shotgun row house in the Five Points section of Wilson, NC, December 14, 1931, grew up in Wayne County, North Carolina, the son of a sharecropper. He was converted in 1949 and began preaching in 1950. In 1955 he entered the ministry of evangelism full time. Since then he has conducted over 2,000 meetings, preached in over 15,000 services.

This booklet was originally published in 1962 under the title "Six Steps to Successful Christian Living". It was written to put a brief summary of foundational truths in the hands of new Believers. Rev. Jackson wanted to help all of the people who were saved under his preaching to get started right and to stay on the right path

When I became a Believer in 1964 someone gave me one of the original "Six Step" booklets. It was a tremendous blessing in the beginning of my life as a Believer. It really helped me get started right. I knew nothing about the Bible when I became a Believer and it gave me the basics in a compact format. My hope is that this booklet will be as great a blessing to you as it was to me.

Jim Cox

Table of Contents

Step 1: Know that You Are Saved	1
Step 2: Walk in God's Truth	6
Step 3: Live a Separated Life	10
Step 4: Practice Prayer Regularly	18
Step 5: Be a Faithful Witness	21
Step 6: Love the Church	2
And Finally	28

STEP 1

KNOW THAT YOU ARE SAVED

You have recently turned to Jesus Christ and trusted Him as your personal Savior. The experience with Him is fresh, real and alive in your soul. Now that Christ has come in, there is peace, satisfaction, and an indescribable joy.

Let's keep it that way.

NOW THAT YOU ARE SAVED

God wants you to always be enthusiastic, happy, zealous and spiritually healthy. He wants your life and testimony to have an impact on others. He doesn't want you to lose interest, grow cold, or become indifferent.

It's God's will that you have victory in your life. He has made the means available to you for overcoming the world, the flesh, and the devil. Take advantage of His provisions.

NAIL DOWN THE FACT THAT YOU ARE SAVED

Six clear suggestions for your spiritual success are listed in Psalm 26. Read the entire passage in your Bible and note the essentials for spiritual growth. If you would live for God successfully, take the steps outlined in this Psalm.

The first verse of Psalm 26 says, "I have trusted also in the Lord; therefore I shall not slide." Remember that salvation is a matter of faith. Assurance comes by trusting in the Lord.

What does it mean to "trust" in the Lord? It simply means to rely upon, have confidence in, commit yourself to, and depend upon the Lord. The synonym in the New Testament is "believe". Salvation is promised to all who believe in (that is, trust in) the Lord Jesus Christ.

These verses will help you nail down the fact that you are saved:

"But as many as received him (Christ), to them he gave the right (or authority) to become the sons of God, even to those who believe (trust, rely, depend) on his name" (John 1:12). If you have trusted in Christ, receiving Him into your life, you have become a son of God.

"For God so loved the world, that he gave his only begotten Son, that whoever believes (trusts) in him should not perish, but have everlasting life" (John 3:16). By trusting in His Son you have everlasting life.

"He who believes (trusts) in him is not condemned: but he who does not believe (trust) is condemned already, because he has not believed (trusted) in the name of the only begotten Son of God" (John 3:18). Are you trusting in the only begotten Son of God? Then you are not condemned.

"He who believes (trusts) on the Son has everlasting life: and he who does not believe (trust) the Son shall not see life; but the wrath of God abides on him" (John 3:36). There are two groups mentioned here: those who trust the Son and those who do not trust Him. The first has life; the second does not have life.

"Truly, truly, I say unto you, He who hears my word, and believes (trusts) in him who sent me, has everlasting life, and shall not come into condemnation; but has passed from death unto life" (John 5:24). By relying upon the Lord, you may be certain that you have life. When you received Christ you were made alive from spiritual death.

"And Jesus said unto them, I am the bread of life: he who comes to me shall never hunger; and he who believes (trusts) in me shall never thirst" (John 6:35). Your thirst is quenched and your hungry soul is satisfied by putting your faith in Him.

"Truly, truly, I say unto you, He who believes (trusts) in me has everlasting life" (John 6:47).

"Jesus answered and said unto them, This Is the work of God, that you believe (trust) in him whom he has sent" (John 6:29).

"There is, therefore, now no condemnation to those who are in Christ Jesus, who walk not after the flesh but after the Spirit." (Romans 8:1)

YOUR FAITH WILL GIVE YOU ASSURANCE

You are not saved by good works (moral, religious, social or otherwise) but by faith in Jesus Christ. If you trust in your own goodness or self- righteousness, you will never have assurance.

"For by grace you are saved through faith; and that not of yourselves: it (salvation) is the gift of God: Not of works, lest any man should boast" (Ephesians 2:8-9).

"And this is the testimony that God has given to us eternal life, and this life is in his Son" (1 John 5:11). Eternal life is a gift from God. You cannot earn it, purchase it, nor merit it. You receive salvation by trusting God and receiving His Son.

"He who has the Son has life; and he who does not have the Son of God does not have life"

(1 John 5:12). Here are the "haves" and the "have nots." If you have Christ, you have life.

It is not correct to say, "I have these wonderful feelings so that I may know I am saved" or "God has given me these amazing experiences so that I may know I am saved." The Bible says, "These things have I written unto you that you may know that you have eternal life." (I John 5:13)

These certain, true, infallible promises are given by God to give you assurance. It is safe to rest your soul upon them. Be sure you are saved by claiming, upon the authority of God's Word, your personal salvation through trusting Jesus Christ.

Your salvation began by faith. It continues by faith. It ends by faith. You must live by faith in Christ, be guided by faith, and die by faith. "Who are kept by the power of God through faith " (1Peter 1:5).

"Trust in the Lord with all your heart: and do not lean on your own understanding. In all your ways, acknowledge him, and he will direct your path," (Proverbs 3:5-6). With this confidence in and reliance upon Christ as Lord and Savior, you have your feet planted firmly on a sure foundation. The writer of Psalm 26 says, "Therefore, I shall not slide" (verse 1).

With this assurance your life as a Believer begins.

STEP 2

WALK IN GOD'S TRUTH

Have you noticed thus far how many Bible verses have been used? There is a reason for this. The Bible is the written revelation of God's truth, and you must learn this truth and live by it if you want to live victoriously.

The writer of Psalm 26 says, "For your lovingkindness is before my eyes: and I have walked in your truth" (verse 3).

Jesus prays to His Father, "Sanctify them through your truth: your word is truth" (John 17:17).

READ THE BIBLE AND LIVE BY IT

The Bible is the Word of God. It is infallibly true. It is God's message to you personally. Love it; learn it; live by it. You cannot walk by God's truth if you are ignorant of it. Study your Bible.

"As newborn babes, desire the sincere milk of the word that you may grow by it" (1 Peter 2:2). You have recently been born into God's family by receiving Christ. As a new-born Believer you need milk and food to grow. That milk is the Word of God. Drink it into your soul.

Jesus said, "Man shall not live by bread alone, but by every word that proceeds out of the mouth of God" (Matthew 4:4). Without food your physical body will become weak and sick. Without spiritual food, which is the word of God, your spirit will become weak and sick. To stay strong, healthy, and growing spiritually you need food. You will find it in the Bible.

HOW TO HANDLE YOUR DOUBTS

When doubts come the only sure and safe way to handle them is with the word of God. The devil may tell you, "You are not saved. You made a mistake. It was all emotion." If he does, just remember that the devil is a liar.

The Bible says, "Whoever shall call upon the name of the Lord shall be saved" (Romans 10:13). You called; God saved.

Jesus said, "He who comes to me I will in no way cast out" (John 6:37). You came; Christ received you.

The devil will probably continue to trouble you about your past sins. He will say. "God didn't forgive them. You don't feel it." Just remember that the Bible says, "As far as the east is from the west, this far he has removed our transgressions from us" (Psalm 103:12).

"If we confess our sins, he is faithful and just to forgive us our sins, and to cleanse us from all unrighteousness." (1 John 1:9).

"Whoever confesses and forsakes them (his sins) shall have mercy". (Proverbs 28:13).

You confessed and turned from your sins; God in mercy forgave and cleansed.

WHAT ABOUT TEMPTATION?

When temptation comes, and it will come, you will find your escape in the Word of God. Christ gained victory over Satan in the wilderness by quoting the Scriptures. He answered the Devil in all three temptations with, "It is written . . ."

God has promised, "There has no temptation overtaken you but such as is common to man: but God is faithful, who will not let you to be tempted above that you are able; but will with the temptation also make a way to escape, that you may be able to bear it" (1 Corinthians 10:13). Your escape is in the Bible, God's word.

THE BIBLE IS YOUR SWORD AND GUIDE

The life of a Believer is warfare. Read Ephesians 6:11-18. You are encouraged to put on the whole armor of God and take "the sword of the Spirit, which is the Word of God." The Bible is your sword. You will need it to fight the good fight of faith.

The Bible is also your guide to live by. What the road map is to the traveler and the compass is to the navigator, the Bible is to you. "Your word is a lamp unto my feet, and a light unto my path . . . Your word have I hid in my heart that I might not sin against you". (Psalm 119:105, 11).

Someone has said of the Bible, "This Book will keep you from sin, or sin will keep you from this Book." Live by its truth. If the Bible says to do something, do it. If the Bible says don't do certain things, don't do them. Remember that the salvation of others will depend upon your sowing the seed which is the Word of God. Learn well the simple passages concerning salvation and pass them on to others.

Read the Gospel of John through several times. Then read the New Testament through at least twice before reading the Old Testament. It would be well to spend much time in the New Testament before going to the Old. The New Testament is more easily understood, and it interprets the Old Testament.
Read the Bible again and again. There is no substitute for this in living victoriously as a Believer.

STEP 3

LIVE A SEPARATED LIFE

You will find further good advice in verses four and five of Psalm 26: "I have not sat with deceitful people, neither will I go in with hypocrites. I have hated the congregation of evil doers: and will not sit with the wicked."

YOU HAVE A CITIZENSHIP

Now that you have become a Believer you are no longer at home in this world. You are a stranger and sojourner making your way to another world. Your citizenship is in heaven.

The Word of God insists that you not participate in the wickedness of this world. Do not compromise with sin or sinners. Your former friends will put pressure on you to join the crowd. Stay away from their bad company. They will only drag you down. Some will suggest that the way to help them is to fellowship with them. Would you say that the way to get a man out of a well is to jump in the well with him? Of course not. You would stand above the well and pull him out.

"Have no fellowship with the unfruitful works of darkness; but rather reprove them"(Ephesians 5:11). You are not only to refrain from participating in such works, but to take a stand against them.

"Be not unequally yoked together with unbelievers: for what fellowship does righteousness have with unrighteousness and what communion does light have with darkness?
. . . Therefore come out from among them, and be separate, says the Lord, and do not touch the unclean thing; and I will receive you, and will be a Father unto you, and you shall be my sons and daughters, says the Lord Almighty" (2 Corinthians 6:14-18). God's people are to be different, separate, holy, a special people.

YOUR LIVING IS TO BE DIFFERENT

"For the grace of God that brings salvation has appeared to all men, teaching us that, denying ungodliness and worldly lusts, we should live soberly, righteously and godly, in this present world; looking for that blessed hope, and the glorious appearing of the great God and our Savior Jesus Christ; Who gave himself for us, that he might redeem us from all iniquity, and purify unto himself a special people, zealous of good works"(Titus 2:11-14).

"Do not love the world, neither the things that are in the world. If any man loves the world, the love of the Father is not in him" (I John 2:15). You are not to be in love with the world, but rather "Set your affection on things above, not on things on the earth" (Colossians 3:2).

"And do not be conformed to this world: but be transformed by the renewing of your mind, that you may prove what is that good, and acceptable, and perfect will of God!" (Romans 12:2). Your life is not to be molded and shaped after the fashion of this world.

"You adulterers and adulteresses, don't you know that the friendship of the world is enmity with God? Whoever therefore will be a friend of the world is the enemy of God!" (James 4:4). The world's friends are God's enemies.

WHAT TO DO IF YOU STUMBLE

This kind of separation will demand that you turn from all that you know to be wrong. Otherwise your conscience will condemn you. "For if our heart condemns us, God is greater than our heart, and knows all things. Beloved, if our heart does not condemn us, then have we confidence toward God" (1 John 3:20-21). The only way to have peace of mind and joy in your heart is to please God.

Make every effort not to sin. "My little children, these things, I write unto you, that you do not sin" (I John 2:1). It is not God's will for you to sin. However, if you do sin, don't throw up your hands in despair and quit. If you stumble, don't stay down. God has made provision to forgive your sins.

"And if anyone sins, we have an advocate with the Father, Jesus Christ the righteous: and he is the covering for our sins" (1 John 2:1-2). Genuine confession and repentance will bring forgiveness and cleansing.

WHAT ABOUT QUESTIONABLE THINGS?

Many times you may be puzzled about things which the Bible does not clearly name as being wrong. You ask yourself, "Should I do this? Or, is it a sin?"

When such a situation faces you, honest answers to the following questions will help you in making a decision:

Is it for the glory of God?

"Whether therefore you eat, or drink, or whatever you do, do all to the glory of God"

(I Corinthians 10:31).

Will it cause others to stumble?

"Therefore, if food makes my brother stumble, I will eat no meat while the world stands, lest I make my brother stumble." (1 Corinthians 8:13).

Do others have a conscience against it?

"But if your brother is grieved with your food, you do not walk in love. Do not destroy him for whom Christ died with your food." (Romans 14:15).

Will it lead to sin?

"Let no man say when he is tempted, I am tempted by God: for God cannot be tempted with evil, neither does he tempt any man: But every man is tempted, when he is drawn away by his own desire, and enticed. Then when desire has conceived, it gives birth to sin: and sin, when it is full grown, brings forth death. (James 1:13-15).

What effect will it have on the unsaved?

"In all things showing yourself a pattern of good works: in doctrine showing integrity, reverence, sincerity, sound speech, that cannot be condemned; that he who is of the contrary part may be ashamed , having no evil thing to say about you" (Titus 2:7-8).

Does it harm my body?

"Don't you know that you are the temple of God, and that the Spirit of God dwells in you? If any man defiles the temple of God, him shall God destroy; for the temple of God is holy, which temple you are" (1 Corinthians 3:16-17). "What? Don't you know that your body is the temple of the Holy Spirit who is in you, whom you have from God, and you are not your own?" (1 Corinthians 6:19).

Will it hinder my testimony?

"Let your light so shine before men, that they may see your good works, and glorify your Father who is in heaven" (Matthew 5:16). "Let no man despise your youth; but be an example to the believers, in word, in conduct, in love, in spirit, in faith, in purity" (1Timothy 4:12).

Does it keep me from my duty?

"Redeeming the time, because the days are evil" (Ephesians 5:16).

"Walk in wisdom toward those who are outside, redeeming the time" (Colossians 4:5).

Is it of faith?

"And he who doubts is condemned if he eats, because he does not eat by faith; for whatever is not by faith is sin" (Romans 14:23).

Does it hurt my own conscience?

"For if our heart condemns us, God is greater than our heart, and knows all things. Beloved, if our heart does not condemn us, then we have confidence toward God" (1 John 3:20-21).

"Holding the mystery of the faith in a pure conscience" (I Timothy 3:9).

What is right with it?

When facing a questionable situation learn to ask, "What is right with it?" rather than "What is wrong with it?"

If by honest answers to these questions you determine that a thing is wrong, have the courage to say with Daniel, "I will not defile myself" -and stick by your convictions.

With this attitude toward sin and the world you may expect opposition. Jesus said, "If the world hates you, you know that it hated me before it hated you. If you were of the world, the world would love its own: but because you are not of the world, but I have chosen you out of the world, therefore the world hates you" (John 15:18-19). After experiencing the hatred of the world even as Jesus had predicted, John then wrote, "Do not marvel, my brothers, if the world hates you" (1 John 3:13).

You are living in the same world which over 1900 years ago nailed Jesus to a cruel cross. Don't expect the approval or cooperation of this wicked world.

YOU HAVE VICTORY THROUGH CHRIST

Stay true to Jesus regardless of the cost, remembering His words, "Blessed are they who are persecuted for righteousness' sake: for theirs is the kingdom of heaven. Blessed are you, when men shall revile you, and persecute you, and shall say all manner of evil against you falsely, for my sake. Rejoice, and be exceedingly glad: for great is your reward in heaven: for they so persecuted the prophets who were before you" (Matthew 5:10-12).

In the face of all persecution be strong, resist the devil, stand firm. Remember that the battle is already won. Christ has gained the victory. Yield your life to Him who lives in your heart. "Greater is he that is in you than he that is in the world"
(1 John 4:4).

STEP 4

PRACTICE PRAYER REGULARLY

Much good counsel is given to you in Psalm 26:6, "So I will go about your altar, O Lord." An altar is a place of prayer and communion with God. It may be at church, at home, or at work. Wherever it is, communion with God is absolutely essential in the life of a Believer.

WHY SHOULD YOU PRAY?

Christ commanded that you pray. "Men should always pray," He said. Prayer played a big part in the life of Jesus. "And when he had sent them away, he departed into a mountain to pray" (Mark 6:46). "He went out into a mountain to pray, and continued all night in prayer to God" (Luke 6:12). In John 17 Jesus poured out His soul to God in earnest prayer for us. Such an example challenges us to pray.

Prayer is necessary for you. You must have supernatural strength to live victoriously as a Believer. This comes through contact with God in prayer.

WHEN SHOULD YOU PRAY?

Jesus prayed night and day. Daniel prayed three times a day. Paul said, "Pray without ceasing"

There is a sense in which we subconsciously may stay in prayer to God all the time. However, you should set aside a definite time daily for private devotions and communion with God.

FOR WHAT SHOULD YOU PRAY?

Pray for anything that you need. James said, "You have not, because you do not ask" (James 4:2). Jesus said, "Ask, and it shall be given to you; seek, and you shall find; knock, and it shall be opened unto you: For everyone who asks receives, and he who seeks finds and to him who knocks it shall be opened" (Matthew 7:7-8).

John put it this way, "And whatever we ask, we receive from him, because we keep his commandments, and do those things that are pleasing in His sight" (1 John 3:22).

Nothing is too great and nothing is too small to pray about. Whether it is an important decision or an insignificant matter take it all to Him in prayer. Finances, sickness, discouragement, burdens, family problems, business, whatever the need, talk it over with God in prayer.

HOW SHOULD YOU PRAY?

This question was asked by the disciples. One said, "Lord, teach us to pray" (Luke 11:1). No one just naturally knows how to pray. Don't be discouraged if you can't word a beautiful prayer. You must learn to pray.

At the beginning, if you can think of nothing more to say to God than the model prayer given by Christ in answer to this request, use it. Think about the words, for in this prayer you will find all the essential elements of sincere, effective praying.

"Therefore, pray like this: Our Father who is in heaven, Hallowed be your name. Your kingdom come. Your will be done on earth, as it is in heaven. Give us this day our daily bread. And forgive us our debts, as we forgive our debtors. And lead us not into temptation, but deliver us from evil: For yours is the kingdom, and the power, and the glory, forever. Amen" (Matthew 6:9-14).

Pray this prayer earnestly to God, adding whatever intercessions the Holy Spirit brings to your mind. Just talk to the Lord in your own language. He will understand.

STEP 5

BE A FAITHFUL WITNESS

Now let's look at Psalm 26:7, "That I may proclaim with the voice of thanksgiving, and tell of all your wondrous works."

This concerns the matter of testifying and witnessing for the Lord Jesus. With gratitude and thanksgiving in your heart, you should proclaim and tell with praise what the Lord has done for you.

WITNESS WITH COURAGE AND BOLDNESS

You are not asked to solve all the theological problems nor answer all the skeptic's questions. Jesus told the man from Gadara, after his deliverance from Satan and sin, "Go home to your friends, and tell them what great things the Lord has done for you" (Mark 5:19).

The Bible says, "He departed, and began to proclaim in Decapolis what great things Jesus had done for him: and all men did marvel" (Mark 5:20).

You should never be ashamed of the Christ who saved you. "For the Scripture says, Whoever believes (trusts) in him shall not be ashamed" (Rom. 10: 11). Always and under any circumstances be ready to tell what the Lord has done for you.

"If you confess with your mouth the Lord Jesus, and believe in your heart that God has raised him from the dead, you shall be saved. For with the heart man believes unto righteousness and with the mouth confession is made unto salvation"
(Romans 10:9-10).

Remember that Christ is representing you to the Father; you are representing Him to the world. "Therefore, whoever shall confess me before men, him I will confess also before my Father who is in heaven. But whoever shall deny me before men, him I will also deny before my Father who is in heaven" (Matthew 10:32-33).

WITNESS FOR CHRIST THROUGH BAPTISM

One way of confessing Christ is by water baptism. As soon as it is conveniently possible you should follow Christ in baptism. In the commission to His disciples, Christ said, "Therefore, go and teach all nations, baptizing them in the name of the Father, and of the Son, and of the Holy Spirit"
(Matthew 28: 19).

Baptism says to the world that you have received Jesus Christ, have died to your old life of sin, and have been resurrected to live in a new life with Him.

A good example to follow is that of the Ethiopian whose story is told in Acts 8:26-39.

THE HOLY SPIRIT GIVES POWER TO WITNESS

"But you shall receive power, after that the Holy Spirit has come upon you: and you shall be witnesses unto me both in Jerusalem and in all Judea, and in Samaria, and unto the uttermost part of the earth" (Acts 1:8).

Through the power of the Holy Spirit who lives in you, Jesus said. "You shall be a witness." Trust Him for leadership, wisdom, and courage that your testimony for Christ may be effective and fruitful, winning others to the Lord.

STEP 6

LOVE THE CHURCH

Another essential part of living successfully as a Believer is found in Psalm 26:8. It deals with your relationship to the church. "Lord, I have loved the habitation of your house, and the place where your honor dwells" (Psalm 26:8).

FIND STRENGTH THROUGH CHURCH ATTENDANCE

Now that you are a child of God, you will enjoy fellowship with others who love the same Christ and share the same joy. This fellowship will be found in an assembly of the Lord's people - a church.

You will gain strength and encouragement from attending church services regularly. That's why the Bible teaches that Believers should meet together for worship and service.

"And let us consider one another to motivate unto love and to good works: Not forsaking the assembling of ourselves together, as the manner of some is; but exhorting one another: and so much the more, as you see the day approaching."
(Hebrews 10:24-25)

IT WILL KEEP YOUR LIGHT SHINING

An old gentleman once told a preacher that he could live close to God at home and never go to church. They were sitting before an open fireplace in the old man's home. The preacher offered no argument He simply took the fire poker and dragged a large, red-hot coal from the fire onto the hearth. A few minutes later he reminded the old man of his statement, pointed to the black, dead coal, and departed.

The illustration is clear. The coals together were still red and glowing. The one alone lacked the heat to maintain its glow. Your life in fellowship with other Believers will stay warm, alive, and shining for Christ. Alone you will grow cold and indifferent. Your light will not shine as brightly. The fire will go out in your spiritual life.

WHAT KIND OF CHURCH SHOULD YOU JOIN?

You need to unite with a good, spiritual, soul winning, missionary minded, gospel preaching church. Consider this matter seriously and pray much, seeking the leadership of the Holy Spirit before making this decision.

Some churches are dead, lifeless, social institutions with a bit of religious ritual and ceremony. They are so akin to freezers that one can imagine icicles dangling from the chandeliers and frost on the pews. That's a poor place for a newborn babe in Christ.

You need a church where the Word of God is preached in the power of the Holy Spirit to feed your soul. You need a church where the fellowship is warm in the Lord to strengthen your life.

In this kind of church you will find a place of service. Whatever talent God has given you, use it for His glory. Do something specific for Christ: sing in a choir, teach a Sunday school class, work as an usher, go on visitation. The Lord may want you in the ministry, or He may call you to be a missionary. In His vineyard He has need of laborers. He can use you.

DEVELOP THE HABIT OF GIVING

You will also want to give of the material wealth entrusted into your hands by the Lord. Those who really love Christ give their money generously and gladly.

Paul said, "He who sows sparingly shall also reap sparingly; and he who sows bountifully shall also

reap bountifully. Every man according as he purposes in his heart, so let him give; not grudgingly, or of necessity: For God loves a cheerful giver"
(2 Corinthians 9:6-7).

By giving you "Lay up treasures in heaven for yourself, where neither moth nor rust corrupts, and where thieves do not break through nor steal: For where your treasure is, there will your heart be also" (Matthew 6:20-21).

The Old Testament standard of giving was the tithe which is giving ten percent unto the Lord. You should go beyond the practice of tithing and give love offerings to the Lord. Remember, He keeps up with that which you spend on yourself, not what you put in the offering plate. All your money belongs to Him. As much of it as possible should be used to support the work of the Lord.

When you love Christ, you will love His people. You will love the house of God. You will attend faithfully because you enjoy the fellowship and worship, not just because you feel responsible. You will be active in working and generous in giving when with all your heart you are in love with Him.

AND FINALLY

Go back through Psalm 26 and underline in your Bible these six essentials in living your life as a Believer. Start taking the six steps now and watch your progress as you climb toward new heights of victory and joy.

"Judge me, O Lord; for I have walked in my integrity: (1) <u>I have trusted also in the Lord, therefore I shall not slide.</u>

Examine me, O Lord, and prove me; try my mind and my heart.

For your lovingkindness is before my eyes: (2) <u>and I have walked in your truth.</u>

(3) <u>I have not sat with deceitful people, neither will I associate with hypocrites.</u>

<u>I have hated the congregation of evildoers; and will not sit with the wicked.</u>

I will wash my hands in innocence: (4) <u>so will I go around your altar, O Lord:</u>

(5) <u>That I may publish with the voice of thanksgiving, and tell of all your wondrous works.</u>

(6) <u>Lord, I have loved the habitation of your house, and the place where your honor dwells.</u>

Do not gather my soul with sinners nor my life with bloody men:

In whose hands is mischief and their right hand is full of bribes.

But as for me, I will walk in my integrity: redeem me, and be merciful unto me.

My foot stands in an even place: in the congregation I will bless the Lord." (Psalm 26)

With this foundation of faith supporting you, you will feel the security and strength of "standing in an even place." From this position you are ready to start climbing the steps toward living successfully as a Believer.

"And the very God of peace sanctify you completely, and I pray God your whole spirit and soul and body be preserved blameless unto the coming of our Lord Jesus Christ" (1 Thess. 5:23).

www.ingramcontent.com/pod-product-compliance
Lightning Source LLC
Chambersburg PA
CBHW050547300426
44113CB00012B/2304